HAPPILY EVER HABITS

A HAPPIER life doesn't happen by accident.
It happens by HABIT!

JASON HARWOOD

HAPPILY EVER HABITS
DO BETTER, FEEL BETTER

For more information, or to book an event, contact :
thejasonharwood@gmail.com
http://www.thejasonharwood.com

Cover design by Hailey Harwood

ISBN - Paperback: 9798386490256

First Edition: February 2023

CONTENTS

CHAPTER 1

introduction

When James Clear, the bestselling author of *Atomic Habits* was a senior in high school, he was tragically hit in the face with a baseball bat and experienced significant medical trauma. As a result, he had to develop new habits necessary to pull himself through that medical trauma and propel him to a successful college baseball career.

As I started studying habits, my initial thought was that to be successful at speaking and teaching about habits, I would have to get hit in the face with a baseball bat. Fortunately for me, I have a son who has played baseball for many years. Unfortunately for me, that same son has also been interested in bodybuilding for many years and at the age of 17 won a statewide bodybuilding competition in his age group. Getting hit in the face with the baseball bat by him would likely kill me! This taught me the first (and most important) lesson of habit creation: your habits must be uniquely yours.

Before I dive into my story, I want to make this point crystal clear, so you don't make the same mistake that I did as you start your journey of creating new habits. James Clear created very specific habits based on his own circumstances and life needs. I created very specific habits based on *my* circumstances and life needs. But the most important lesson is that my habits and James Clear's habits probably look nothing alike. One of the early mistakes that I made and that I have seen hundreds of other people make is that they develop habits based on recommendations from other people. It is common to see habits that work for other people and try to match them perfectly. But the habits that are successful for others are built on the life circumstances and situations of *that person*. You are not James Clear, your neighbor, your boss, or your best friend. You're not the influencer that you look at on Instagram every day, nor are you the hundred people that you follow on Facebook. Trying to match their habits will lead you to greater unhappiness and frustration.

Don't go out looking to get hit in the face by a baseball bat just because somebody else did. Just as importantly, don't try to match someone else's health or financial patterns, personal development goals or career success, material achievements, or relationships with God or family members. Choosing to mirror or focus on another person's habits will always lead to personal disappointment because your habit story is different from my habit story or James Clear's habit story. I was not hit in the face with a baseball bat, but I got to my own place of remarkable personal pain that forced my unique habit formation. In telling my story, I hope that it might resonate with you – not so you will try to match your story to mine and then match your habits to mine, but so that you can see the pattern of personal development in yourself that will then lead you to the creation of your own powerful habits.

I have talked to and interviewed many people about habits who had circumstances like James Clear. Never have I talked to anyone who's been hit in the face, but I've talked to many people who have been in car accidents, had medical emergencies, or a sudden health reversal. I have talked to people who have had a terrible diagnosis, been fired from jobs, or experienced the tragic end of a personal relationship that changed their world. In some cases, these things happen with such incredible speed that it's almost like turning off the light. One moment, it's bright and clear, and the next moment it's pitch dark. Often, the pain of pitch darkness is the reason people suddenly decide to make a change in life.

That isn't what happened to me. And it isn't what happens to most people I talk to. Maybe your story is more like mine.

Life is a Sunset

My own experience did not resemble turning off a light. Instead, my experience resembled a sunset. When you're sitting outside at sunset, you don't notice the exact moment that it becomes dark or the exact moment when you go from being able to see to not being able to see. It all happens very gradually. Similarly, the darkness that came into my life happened gradually. There was no light switch where one moment it was bright and the next moment, I found myself in emotional darkness. I can't tell you the exact day, hour, or moment that the darkness started. I do know it gradually got darker, a little bit at a time.

I want to tell you my story because I think for many of you it will sound much like your story: a gradual journey into the darkness of unhappiness. And more importantly, I want to share how I used habits to come out of it.

I went to college, got a degree, and got a job that I was really excited about. I enrolled in graduate school to get my master's degree to increase my education and along with it my earning potential. I made a couple of job changes and climbed a bit of the corporate ladder. Throughout this time, I was married and had children. I lived in a nice house in a nice neighborhood, drove nice cars, and went on occasional, nice vacations. Yet, strangely, my life seemed to be slipping deeper and deeper into unhappiness and discontent. I would wake up in the morning and the first thought that would pop into my head was one of despair for the day. Do I really have to go through this day again? Of course, the answer was always yes. I would then have to go through the day, looking forward to the time I could lie down and go back to sleep from the moment I woke up until the moment I went to bed. Strangely, going back to sleep was one of the things I most looked forward to throughout the day. I would go to work, interact with my children and my wife, and mow my lawn – all the while slipping deeper and deeper into the darkness of unhappiness and pain.

One morning was different. I remember waking up next to my beautiful wife, putting my feet down on the carpet in my nice house, sitting on the edge of my nice bed that my wife had picked out. I knew that I had to go upstairs and wake up my wonderful children and help get them ready for school; I knew that I would then jump into my nice car and drive to my nice job, passing through my nice neighborhood in my safe and wonderful community.

For some reason, at that moment I finally decided I had had enough pain. I looked around and felt as though I were in a dark room with all the lights turned off. My life was dark, my thoughts were dark, my emotions were dark. I was in a dark place. It didn't happen suddenly like getting hit in the face with a baseball bat. It had happened gradually over several years. If someone had asked me how I was doing, I would have said fine. If someone had asked me to describe my life, I would have said I was floating. I was just floating through life – and that was the problem. My life was fine, but I was floating deeper into darkness – gradually, step by step, day by day.

In that moment, I was in as much need of a life and habit transformation as James Clear was the day he got hit in the face with the baseball bat. I literally could not continue to live in the circumstances I had created. It was not about moving, changing jobs, or changing major relationships in my life. It was not about changing my children or anyone else around me. It all came down to exchanging the habits that had gotten me to where I was for the habits that would get me to where I wanted to be. I was not in this dark place in my life due to anyone else's behavior or habits. I was in this place in my life because of my habits. I had gotten myself there and if anyone was going to get me out of that darkness, it was going to be me. It was not going to happen like a light switch where I could have one burst of momentous activity and suddenly be or feel different. No single burst of motivation would move me from darkness to light. I had slipped into darkness slowly, methodically, day by day, and action by action. I knew the only way out was slowly, methodically, day by day, and action by action.

This is where the habit principle becomes so important. You can't possibly find success matching and mirroring someone else's habits because their habits are based on their pain and their level of darkness. Your habits must be built on your pain and the level of darkness and unhappiness you experience, the kind of person you aspire to be, and what you want to accomplish in your life. Whether you are aware of it or not, your habits consistently move you every single day, either deeper into darkness or further into the light of happiness.

Let's look at this idea of habits moving you closer to or further away from what you want, using James Clear as an example. James Clear started making significant habit changes and learning about the process of habit creation because of his tragic experience of getting hit in the face with the baseball bat. Most of us will not have that kind of dramatic experience and, for better or worse, that puts us in a much different place.

Sometimes it's easier to make a change when we are forced to like James Clear was. For example, when somebody is diagnosed with diabetes, they usually make immediate dietary changes in their life that they may have been unsuccessfully trying to make for years. I have seen women who find out they are pregnant and immediately eliminate smoking or drinking when they had previously been unable to change these habits. In these cases, outside factors like a diabetes diagnosis or becoming pregnant force behavior change.

But what about those of us who don't have outside factors influencing us to change? What if you just wake up day after day in a life you're unhappy with? Nothing is really wrong, but you feel unfulfilled. You have so many blessings and gifts and yet inside you feel empty and unhappy. There isn't a dramatic outside factor; instead, you can take accountability and responsibility into your own hands. You can choose the day and time that you will decide to live differently – to live better and be happier.

Today can be the day you decide that, from here on out, every tomorrow is going to be a bit brighter and that every morning can be an opportunity to make positive changes.

I hope this book serves as an invitation to you to take a mental "hit to the face" and choose to live better, live happier and live up to your full potential. It doesn't have to be for a dramatic reason, it can just be because you woke up today and decided that tomorrow will be better because you've had enough "fine" days. You've had enough of drifting in the darkness and you are ready to compel yourself to live better by taking action *today*. You are what you do *today* and you can decide today to be a person who lives a little bit happier each day, starting now.

I have come to learn that life is not a series of tasks or accomplishments. It is not a journey of accumulation or trying to move up a ladder. Our daily habits are pointing us in a direction; in fact, everything we do every day is pointing us in a certain direction. All the habits of your life have led you in the direction of where you are right now. If you were to continue in your current daily habits, not changing anything at all, the direction is set and will not change. The only way to change your life is to address your daily habits and start shifting direction. Again, for some people, it's like a light switch. You're going along in one direction in your life and then suddenly, you're hit in the face with the baseball bat. You crash your car, you lose your job, you get divorced, or you get a terrible health prognosis. In these moments, your direction changes drastically.

But these dramatic moments that force change are rare. For so many of us, the direction is slow and steady and almost imperceptible. And that's the challenge. You can't point to a single day and say, "That was the day I started slipping into darkness." You can't point to a single day and say, "That is the day where my unhappiness started." Why not? Because the direction of your daily habits slowly leads you into a state where you are unhappy or unfulfilled, where there is a gap between whom you wanted to be and who you are, what you wanted to accomplish and what you have actually done, whom you wanted to become and who you actually became. This is where we all start. We start with the concept of how we see ourselves because this will set the direction for today and the opportunity for direction tomorrow. This is the beginning of the change of habits.

On taking accountability for our attitudes and behaviors:

"People aren't living their best life because I think primarily it's this victim mentality. It's this searching outside of ourselves for a reason why we can't be successful. 'It's because of the way I was raised.' 'It's because of my economic status.' 'Oh, it's because of this.' And we look outside ourselves for all the reasons. But once we can take in this radical accountability for ourselves, you realize everything is your fault, which is great.

When you've got a great life, you're like, look at all this I've accomplished and all these wonderful things I have. I did that. I'm proud of myself, but I think a lot of times people, when you say, 'Hey, it's your fault' they feel attacked. They feel shame. [Because] we all have that thing that we did once that we just cringe. You got that internal 'ick' like, 'I can't believe I did that.' If you let that compound over your whole life, I think that keeps you from taking radical accountability for what you've done and then once you can start to realize everything's your fault, it empowers you to start making the changes that you want to see in your own life. So that's the 'everything is your fault' mentality."

– Lia Bliss, from the Happily Ever Habits podcast

When I was slipping into darkness, I saw myself as a person who was unhappy in my marriage. I saw myself as a person who was not very effective as a father. I saw myself as a person who had capped out my potential in my career. I saw myself as a person who would never find the level of happiness and fulfillment I had wanted when I was young and ambitious. Because I saw myself as that type of person, that was my *direction*. It was a self-fulfilling prophecy because the way I saw myself and the habits I had in place set that direction in my mind and my life. My habits and self-awareness slowly started to align that morning as I was sitting on my nice bed in my nice house next to my beautiful wife, ready to go wake up my wonderful children. I decided at that moment to see differently. The power of that moment is that it was a simple decision with unalterable consequences. That simple decision to see myself as someone who has a happy relationship with his wife, who is a successful father, who eats healthy, exercises, has financial stability, finds satisfaction in a career and hobbies and who finds ways to contribute to the world in ways that bring me happiness and fulfillment changed the direction of my life.

That day, I decided I was no longer going to fixate on the accumulation of things, but rather on my acts of service to others. It was a shift into seeing myself as the person I wanted to be – the person I knew I could become –and developing the small daily habits that would get me there. Knowing that small daily habits had gotten me into that dark place reinforced that it was small daily habits that would get me to where I wanted to be. Immediately, my behaviors started changing. As soon as I saw myself as a person who could have a happy relationship with his spouse, my behavior towards my wife changed. As soon as I saw myself as a person who could be a successful father, my interactions with my kids changed. The same thing happened at work, in my health and my financial stability.

Now, I'll be honest. My story is not a rags-to-riches story. I haven't suddenly doubled or tripled my income. I haven't suddenly gone from the brink of divorce and total disaster in all my relationships to now being perfectly happy. I still have struggles and difficulties. I still make about the same amount of money I made before. But my focus has changed to looking at life as the direction of my character rather than the accumulation of things. I am more charitable and giving. I am happier in my relationships, healthier in my body, and healthier in my spirit. It was not one grand action, one burst of motivation, or one weekend course on a Zoom conference that helped me to get there. It started with a mindset shift that was tied to daily, consistent changes in habits.

It is my desire that this book will help you create new habits that help you become the person you want to be. We will start by going through the process of a mindset shift and then talk about why habits are so important and how much of our lives are determined by them. And then I will give you the three simple keys to creating and sustaining habits – the habits that will make you happier; the habits that will help you feel more fulfilled; the habits that will help you be healthier in your mind, in your character, in your body, in your spirit; habits that will make you healthier in your relationships, your character and growth and in your charity, kindness, and interactions with others. I am excited to be on this journey with you because of what it did for me and what I know it can do for you.

What habit will you build? You might have some ideas. The next chapter will guide you through picking the habit that will bring you the most personal happiness!

Your Happily Ever After doesn't come because you hope for it. It comes when you create your own Happily Ever Habits!

CHAPTER 2

the importance of gratitude

In the next few chapters, we are going to get into the science of how to create habits and particularly how to get them to stick. But before we do, I want to get you started on a habit that can have a significant impact on your happiness right away. In fact, I have already mentioned this habit a few times. I want this book to have an impact on you as quickly as possible. So, before we dive into fully understanding how to create your own habits, I want to spend some time suggesting one particular habit that has had a significant impact on me and that research shows will have a significant impact on you as well. You see, we want to change our lives from the sun setting to the sun rising, from gradually getting darker to continually getting lighter.

How do we do that? Well, the first step is to determine the direction we're facing. If you are facing east, you're far more likely to see a sunrise; if you're facing west, you're far more likely to see a sunset. Maybe many of you relate to this.

I would wake up in the morning and one of the first thoughts that would pop into my head would be that I didn't want to get through that day. That set the direction of my feet, my mind, my heart, and my emotions facing toward a sunset. Many of you probably experience the same thing. You wake up, you grab your phone and you're immediately thrown into emails, text messages, work messages. Maybe you immediately look at social media and start falling into a trap of comparing your day and your life to everyone else's. And before you're even aware of it, you have set your feet to the west, to the sunset. Your mind and mental state are driving you in the direction of that sunset rather than a sunrise.

I came across a poem that really helped me understand this and helped remind me of what I needed to do every day. The poem is from Ella Wheeler Wilcox entitled *Tis the Set of the Sail*. She said:

One ship sails East,

And another West,

By the self-same winds that blow,

'Tis the set of the sails

And not the gales,

That tells the way we go.

Like the winds of the sea

Are the waves of time,

As we journey along through life,

'Tis the set of the soul,

That determines the goal,

And not the calm or the strife.

So many mornings I would remind myself it's the set of my sails, not the gales that determine which way I go. It's how I start my day that sets my sails. It's the direction that I face at the beginning of the day that makes a difference. This is true for you, too. How you start your morning has an impact on the rest of your day, and each of those days strung together creates the collective direction of your life – whether you are facing the sun setting or rising.

I love the quote from John Wooden who said, "Things work out best for those who make the best of the way things work out." Similar to the poem that I love from Ella Wheeler Wilcox, it reminded me that whether I am experiencing sunset or sunrise has little to do with the circumstances around me and everything to do with how I choose to make value judgments about what's going on.

This new way of thinking led me to the habit that has had the biggest impact on my overall happiness, mental health and emotional wellness, and that is gratitude journaling. Like me, you've probably heard about gratitude journaling before. Like me, you've probably heard somewhere that it is a good idea. Maybe you've even started some gratitude journals like me. You may have a journal that has two or three days of positive statements followed by a six-month break and then three or four days of positive journal entries with a three-month break and then another week of positive journal entries. I wanted to incorporate gratitude journaling into my daily practice and had never been successful doing it until I started applying the principles that I'm about to teach you later in this book. But I want to get you started even before you fully understand all the principles because this habit will make the most difference.

A 2017 research experiment done by Joshua Brown and Joel Wong from the University of California, Berkeley found that there are a few significant positive impacts that come from gratitude journaling. The first is that gratitude "disconnects us from toxic negative emotions and the ruminating that often accompanies them." That's the set of the sail. When we wake up and start with gratitude journaling, we are able to disconnect from toxicity, fear of missing out (FOMO), and comparing ourselves to others. We're able to disconnect from negativity.

14

We set our sail for the day.

Those first few minutes every day determine how we are going to mentally approach today. Second, expressing gratitude helps even if we don't share it with others. You don't have to tell people. You can write it down in a simple gratitude journal. A third impact that Brown and Wong found is that gratitude journaling has a positive impact that increases over time. So, the first day that you write in your gratitude journal, you don't see a significant impact, but the more you do it, the more the positive impact increases.

Do it for a week and the impact is greater. Do it for a month and the impact increases. Do it for six months and your outlook on life changes. In fact, your *life* changes. It might take a few days, a week, or a month before you really start to see an impact, but if you set your sails towards gratitude and positivity every morning for a month, you will notice the difference.

Finally, one of the most important and interesting points that Brown and Wong found is that when we write down things that we are grateful for, it trains our brain to become more aware of things for which to be grateful. This is a powerful mental reality that we all deal with: our brains take in far more information than we can ever process. There is too much input for our brain to process, so it naturally filters out a lot of what we see, what we hear, and what we experience.

Those filters in our brains are developed over time as we determine for ourselves what's important and what is dangerous, focusing on things that *we have determined* are important or dangerous. The more frequently you write gratitude statements, the more consistently you communicate with your mind that gratitude and positivity are important, the more consistently your mind will notice things to be grateful for.

It's a strange phenomenon but has been proven time and time

again. One fun exercise you can do with your family or even by yourself to test this out is the color challenge. Have your family sit together and write down five things that they notice around the room, then have everybody share what they noticed.

Then state a specific color like red and see how many things they can write down that are the color red. They will notice more red items after you say the word red than they noticed before you said red. Initially, they were noticing everything in the room; as soon as you say "red," they start noticing red objects.

That's what happens in your brain. As soon as you tell your brain it's important to start recognizing things for which to be grateful, you will immediately notice more things and that starts to compound and build. You have set your sails towards sunrise and you start noticing things differently. As John Wooden says, you start making the best of what happens instead of making the worst of what happens.

Gratitude journaling can have a significant impact. Now, I'm going to walk you through step by step in the next few chapters how to make gratitude journaling a consistent part of your life. Right now, I'm going to give you the steps and then later discuss the reason behind these steps.

To start with, pick a notebook, pad, or even just a piece of paper and get a pen or pencil that you like writing with. Set them where it is easy for you to remember to use them. Next, pick an action that you do consistently in the morning. Maybe it's having your cup of coffee, taking a shower, getting dressed, or any other morning action. Decide right now to tie gratitude journaling to that morning action.

Maybe your morning looks like getting your morning cup of coffee, grabbing that notepad off your dining room table, and (while drinking your morning coffee) writing three things you're grateful for before you start scrolling Instagram.

Maybe it's setting your notepad in the bathroom and, before taking a shower, you quickly write down three things you're grateful for and then jump in the shower. Maybe it's leaving that notepad in your closet and when you come in to get dressed, you quickly write down three things that you're grateful for and then get dressed. The key is that writing down things you're grateful for should take you less than two minutes.

At the end of this chapter, I am going to give you a series of gratitude journaling prompts to get your mind started on writing down three things that you're grateful for. You can use these prompts if you ever feel stuck or simply can't think of three things to be grateful for.

As you go throughout the day, you'll start to notice things that will cause you to think, "Maybe I'll write that down on my list tomorrow." As you set your sails towards gratitude and positivity, you will notice more things for which to be grateful. You will disconnect from toxic negative thoughts and emotions and, rather than experiencing negativity, stress, comparison, frustration, or being overwhelmed with the tasks of the day, you will start with a simple act of writing down three things you're grateful for. That gets your morning – every morning – started in a much more positive way.

The next few chapters will explain exactly why I told you to set up your gratitude journaling habit in exactly this way. But I encourage you to start on the habit *today*, even before getting through the next few chapters, so you can start experiencing the positive impact of this important habit.

Gratitude journal prompts

These are all in threes and should all be written in your gratitude journal. Over time you will come up with your own prompts!

- Three things you are grateful for that move you out of your comfort zone.
- Three mistakes you are grateful you made and what you learned from them.
- Three things related to your life's purpose or passion that make you grateful to be alive.
- Three things you do with some discipline that you are grateful for.
- Three things you are working toward that you are grateful for.
- Three things you are grateful for that are helping you change or grow.
- Write "I'm grateful I have the power to..." and fill in the blanks. Focus on what you can control.
- Three things you are grateful for that you want to focus on this week. "I am grateful for and will focus on..."
- Three things you are grateful for in the future tense. This is something you are grateful will happen, even if it is aspirational.
- Three things in your environment that you are grateful for.
- Three things you can do for others that you are grateful for.
- Three things that you are grateful to love in your life.
- Three parts of your life story that you are grateful for.
- Three statements of what you see as your purpose.
- Three things you are grateful for that you like to do just for yourself.
- Three things that challenge you that you need to start saying "no" to.
- Three times you were grateful to have the time to spend with loved ones.
- Three things you are successful at that you are grateful for.

- Three things that are beautiful or make your life beautiful.
- Three things you are grateful you have time to do.
- Three flaws that you are grateful to keep working on. Give yourself the grace to keep trying!
- Three people you haven't talked to this month that you are grateful for. Today might be a good time to reach out to them!
- Three things that happened yesterday (or last month or last year) that you are grateful for.

CHAPTER 3

aligning new habits with your core values

Now that you have established your first new habit of gratitude journaling, before we dive into how to create habits we need to spend some time on what habits to develop. This book could take a practical approach and just focus, for example, on how to floss your teeth more consistently. (I actually have the exact habit hack formula for how to floss your teeth every single day. I use it and haven't had to lie to the dentist about flossing since I started.) Or I could focus on habits like eating more vegetables, eating less sugared cereal, how to drink more water instead of pop.

The habit process that I'm going to teach you will help you in each of those areas, and many more. But when I was sitting in the darkness of my own unhappiness, I wasn't looking for a solution to flossing my teeth or doing more pushups, or eating more vegetables. I was looking for a solution for how to become a different, happier version of myself. I wanted to develop the core characteristics that would bring me joy, not just fewer cavities. So, I encourage you to focus on the same thing in your life. Trust me, when you want to floss more regularly, eat more vegetables, and get more sleep, the habit process I will teach you *will* come into play, and you can employ the same system to get those types of results.

My son, who just turned 20 recently asked me to tell him the one habit I thought he should start working on. He said, "Pretend you're not my dad. Pretend you're just the habit coach. What's the one habit I should start implementing immediately?" And I told him the same thing I am now telling you. The answer is that it depends on what core character traits you want to develop that will help you become a happier, more fulfilled person.

When I was sitting on my bed in a dark place, I was able to reflect on my life and recall times when I felt the happiest and most fulfilled. I thought through times when I felt the light of joy come into my life and I started to identify common characteristics of all those times. For me, I find incredible joy in doing acts of service and showing kindness and generosity to others, so I made that a core character trait for me. I find joy in learning and reading, so that's another core character trait for me. I also wanted to be a more humble and grateful person because the humble and grateful people that I know seem the happiest, so I made humility and gratitude core character traits for me. I wanted to live authentically to whom I wanted to be, so I made integrity a core character trait for me.

Now, I want to invite you to spend a few minutes going through the same mental exercise I used to define who I wanted to be so I could then establish the habits I would need to help me get there. Ask yourself the following questions:

(1) When in your life have you felt most fulfilled?

(2) When in your life have you felt internal happiness that was not contingent on any external factor?

(3) When in your life have you felt yourself growing and the joy that comes from growth?

(4) Who in your life do you look at as a model of happiness and what are some of the character traits you most closely associate with them?

Take a few minutes and write down specific times, places, and/or situations that made you implicitly happy. What you'll start to see is the development of consistent patterns. If you are stuck and truly can't think of anything, you are more than welcome to borrow some of my core character traits to build some of yours. Mine include gratitude, generosity, learning, humility, and integrity. You can also go to my website (www.thejasonharwood.com) or use the QR code below to download the *Happily Ever Habits Guide* which contains seven core values and worksheets on how to tie those values to your daily habits.

Scan this QR code to get your Happily Habits Guide!

Whatever core values you choose, remember that they must be important to you. They must help you feel like you are working toward living your best self.

Far too often, we live out the best version of what we think others want us to be. Today, I want you to identify the best version of whom *you* want to be. Don't identify a core value and then develop a habit because you think somebody else would like it or because you think it will help you make more money. This whole process is meant to lead you to feel connected to the best version of yourself.

I will show you how I developed small habits in each of my core character trait focus areas that I do on a daily or sometimes weekly basis: learning every day, showing gratitude every day, actions to try to be humble every day, actions to connect with my authentic self to make sure I'm living a life of integrity every day. These habits helped me become the best version of myself and to look forward to each day because I knew I would grow to become a better person. I stopped dreading every day. I stopped living out the hopes, dreams, and expectations of other people, or the responsibilities that other people had placed upon me. I started to live true to myself.

I invite you to do the same. If you haven't yet, stop reading or listening pick up a piece of paper and a pencil, and think about the questions above. Spend 10 minutes visualizing and writing it out. Making that list will help you define the habits that can actually bring you happiness and impact your whole life. The most fascinating part of this process is that your new habits will have a spill-over impact, which means that if you work on being more grateful, the impact of that will spill over into other parts of your life.

For example, when I act in a humbler way my relationships get better, my work life gets better, and my health gets better. There's almost no part of my life that is unaffected. I'm focusing on becoming the best version of myself, which enables me to not only live happier and feel more fulfilled but to show up as a better version of myself in every area of my life. The promise is that when you focus on core character traits and build habits that make you happier, you will find positive results in all aspects of your life. Once you have your core character traits identified, it's time to start the journey of creating a habit in each of those areas.

MASTERMIND ASSIGNMENT

Before we get started on the elements necessary to successfully create and maintain new habits, take a few minutes right now to identify one to three core values that you want to support with new habits. Circle one of the values below (these are the core values we focus on in the Happily Ever Habits Mastermind) or write one of your own in the spaces provided. For each core value, I have provided a definition to help you determine where to focus.

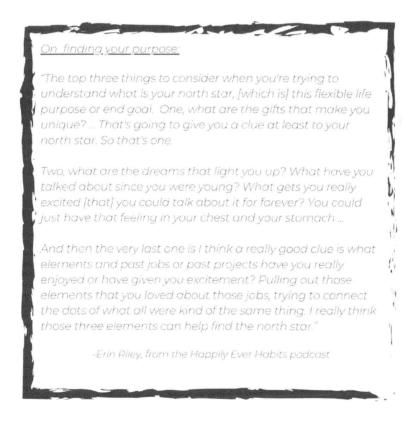

On finding your purpose:

"The top three things to consider when you're trying to understand what is your north star, [which is] this flexible life purpose or end goal. One, what are the gifts that make you unique? ... That's going to give you a clue at least to your north star. So that's one.

Two, what are the dreams that light you up? What have you talked about since you were young? What gets you really excited [that] you could talk about it for forever? You could just have that feeling in your chest and your stomach ...

And then the very last one is I think a really good clue is what elements and past jobs or past projects have you really enjoyed or have given you excitement? Pulling out those elements that you loved about those jobs, trying to connect the dots of what all were kind of the same thing. I really think those three elements can help find the north star."

-Erin Riley, from the Happily Ever Habits podcast

◆BELIEF: A state or habit of mind in which trust or confidence is placed in some person (especially yourself!) or thing.

◆INTEGRITY: Firm adherence to a code of values.

◆KNOWLEDGE: The range and depth of one's information or understanding.

◆SELF-CONTROL: The ability to control one's emotions and desires or the expression of them in one's behavior, especially in difficult situations.

◆GRATITUDE: Being thankful; readiness to show appreciation for and to return kindness.

◆CHARITY: Generosity and helpfulness especially toward the needy or suffering.

◆HUMILITY: Showing that you do not think of yourself as better than other people. A modest view of one's importance.

◆OTHER (write in your own core value): _____

Scan this QR code for a
video walkthrough of
the
Pick Your Core Values
Activity

Your Happily Ever After doesn't come because you hope for it. It comes when you create your own Happily Ever Habits!

CHAPTER 4

the three components of habits

Did you know that habits make up 80% to 90% of the actions you take in your life? The pattern by which habits are created and sustained is consistent and biological. Habits are made up of three components. In his bestselling book *The Power of Habit,* Charles Duhigg talks about the habit circle that every person creates and recreates, whether subconsciously or consciously. The first step is that a cue or trigger is initiated. This trigger kicks your mind into habit mode, and your mind walks you through the same consistent habit pattern followed by the reward that you have found as a consistent outcome of that behavior.

Simply put, according to Duhigg the three parts of every habit are the cue, the behavior, and the reward. It's easy to see this. When you talk about eating food, you get a cue that you are hungry. You eat food and you get the reward of being full. One of the challenges is that these cues are often connected to unwanted behaviors.

For example, I often have a cue that kicks in at about 10 p.m. that it's time to eat. This is not because I'm hungry or need additional food to sustain life. It's just a habit that I have developed of late-night eating. So, the cue kicks in as "normal" late at night and my body expects me to eat, which is followed by the reward of feeling satisfied. Unfortunately, late-night eating is usually unhealthy food like cereal or cookies, or ice cream, but no matter how hard I fight it, the cue always kicks in. Knowing that this is the consistent and predictable pattern of all habit formation is the first step in making changes. Because if you want to make changes in your habits, you must impact at least one of these components of the habit behavior. You must impact the cue to either change or eliminate it, you must impact the behavior that you engage in when you are prompted with that cue, or you must change the result or reward.

As mentioned earlier, your brain wants you to continue in your existing habit behaviors. Biologically your brain desires a series of consistent cues so that as soon as your brain detects the cue, it can slip into habit mode. This preserves energy as you are consistently engaging in behaviors that your brain knows are safe and reliable and that it can perform repeatedly with little additional energy spent on learning new behaviors. Again, this biological process is great if you have healthy and positive habits and detrimental if you have habits that do not lead to your long-term health or happiness because your mind will continually try to drive to those same habits and will resist you as you try to make changes. Being aware of this pattern helps you in combating undesirable habit outcomes. Also important to note is that research has indicated that once a habit is created, it is nearly impossible to eliminate that habit. It is always there. What you can do is start to replace an existing habit with an alternative habit. You will never eliminate the connections in your brain, also known as neural pathways, of the previous habit, but you can create a new habit based on old cues.

I saw this happen with my dad many decades ago when he decided to quit smoking. As part of the program he went through, he tried to identify the cues that happened just before smoking. Then he would identify new behaviors to engage in to replace smoking and try to connect with the positive results of those behaviors. For example, he would often smoke immediately after dinner. Finishing dinner was his cue; he would then engage in behavior – the pattern of smoking – and then get the reward, which was the nicotine hit and the other physical and emotional impacts of smoking. He replaced smoking after dinner with going on a walk. After experiencing the physical and emotional benefits of going on a walk, over time he was able to create a new pattern in his mind that when the cue of finishing dinner happened, his mental mode would slip to going on a walk rather than smoking a cigarette.

This same process works for each of us with our own existing cues. The rest of this book is dedicated to the three simple rules necessary to work within this pattern of cue, behavior, and reward. Those three rules are to start small, make it easy, and celebrate small wins. These rules work to start behaviors or habits that you want to engage in and to eliminate behaviors or habits that you want to change. The keys to understanding this are to (1) remember that your brain will fight you in this endeavor because it wants you to continue to engage in the habits you're already engaging in, and (2) realize that it will be impossible for you to completely eliminate those habits, but it is entirely possible to create new habits that override the existing habit pattern. The best part is that rewiring your habits is systematic so that you can get the results you want without having to rely on the inconsistencies of luck or on unpredictable bursts of motivation. We will instead focus on *consistent habits* so that your results and outcomes are consistent and predictable.

MASTERMIND ASSIGNMENT

Throughout the day, notice cues that are tied to your behaviors and capture three of them here. By noticing cues, you notice your existing (subconscious) habits and are then able to change them.

CUE 1: _____

CUE 2: _____

CUE 3: _____

Scan this QR code for a video walkthrough of the
Become Aware of
Your Cues Activity

Your Happily Ever After doesn't come because you hope for it. It comes when you create your own Happily Ever Habits!

CHAPTER 5

wired for habits

Now that you are ready to make every day a little bit brighter and get a little bit closer to your goals, let's talk about how to do it. When I was sitting on my nice bed in my nice house next to my beautiful wife, ready to go wake up my wonderful children, I decided it was time to make my life brighter and happier. I knew this wouldn't happen through a single burst of action or extreme motivation. What comes to mind as the type of single-burst action you can take that has a lasting impact on happiness? It's not something even as dramatic as winning the lottery or as significant as becoming a parent for the first time. These are both very exciting and life-altering but having become a parent multiple times I know from experience that the immediate impact of these events eventually wears off.

Maybe it's buying a new car, buying a new house, getting a new job, getting a promotion, or moving to a new town. All these events can result in singular exciting bursts of positive energy, but they do not result in long-lasting impact on overall happiness. In fact, when looking at personal finances, research studies show that there is a diminishing return on an increase in income. Once your basic needs are met there is a diminishing emotional return on the financial increase. In other words, a 25% raise is not going to make you 25% happier. Research also shows that the real key to lasting, significant happiness is not in single life events but in the long-term impact of building a life of significant contribution to others. This is *personal meaning* and personal meaning and satisfaction start with building your core character.

In my personal example, as I slipped further and further into darkness, I learned that the material objects and activities in my life were not what was out of line. It was not the house or the car or the career. I had the house and the car and the fulfilling career. I was doing great. It was not the kids – I have seven of them. There was no external accomplishment that I needed to help me get out of the darkness. What was out of alignment was my inner core or character, which had slowly gotten out of alignment day by day, step by step. And it was only day by day and step by step that I could get myself back in alignment. That is the true power of habit because habit is not based on motivation. It's not a one-time boost of incredible energy and excitement. ***Habit is the slow, consistent discipline and growth of the right behaviors that lead to a life of meaning, achievement, and significance.***

On how we are wired for habits:

"Habits [are] a way of ingraining a behavior and an attitude into who you are. So, when something becomes who you are, you're no longer using willpower ... What that means is I don't use willpower to exercise. Some days when I don't feel like it, I may leverage that muscle of willpower, but it's not a battle because it's fundamentally part of my identity and ultimately your habits and what you do will serve your identity and how you see yourself. That's [how] human beings are designed ... We have a cognitive dissonance when we're misaligned with how we see ourselves and [when] the habits and the behaviors ... are misaligned, we don't work very well. ...

We are what we do, not what we think about ourselves. You see, this is why habits are as unsexy as they are. If you ... just look at someone's habits and you remove the person and you just were to look at a timeline of someone's day and record their habits ... that'll give you the picture of who they are. Some may argue with me that ... [a] human being is a mix of ... thought [and] emotion. But in the practical sense, if you're talking about performance orientation, we are what we do, not what we think or what we feel."

-- RJ Singh, from the Happily Ever Habits podcast

And just so I'm not misunderstood, when I say achievement, I don't mean external achievement. I mean the achievement that can only come through having reached a greater sense of self and purpose. What makes habits so important in achieving this greater sense of self and purpose? One of the reasons habits are so important is because they take up so much of your day. As I mentioned earlier, research indicates that your day is 80% to 90% habit, from the moment you wake up in the morning to the moment you go to bed. Your morning routine is a habit. Your showering routine is a habit. You brush your teeth as a habit, you get dressed as a habit. You drive to work or drive the kids to school based on habit. If you go to work, you work as a habit. If you're at home, you do the same consistent things. You probably empty the dishwasher in a very habitual pattern. You wash your clothes as a form of habit, you vacuum your house as a form of habit, and you watch TV as a form of habit. You exercise as a form of habit. Nearly every aspect of your life is a habit.

Your brain is biologically wired for habits. It wants you to engage in habits because habits keep it alive for several reasons. Once you do something and you don't die, that is very attractive to your brain because your brain wants to keep you alive. So, if you drive to work a certain way and you don't get in an accident and if it's the best way to get to work, that clicks in your brain as something safe, reliable, and should be repeated. You got the outcome you wanted (arrived at work safely and on time), so your brain will biologically push you to those behaviors because they save energy.

When you slip into unattractive habits, sometimes it's simply your brain trying to keep you alive. For example, you know that if you don't go running today, you won't die. But when you DO go running and you literally feel like you could die, your brain doesn't like that. Your brain wants to keep you alive, so it tells you not to go running – because when you do go running, you think and feel as if you are going to die, and your brain says don't do that. Coming up with excuses to cancel your run may be an obvious example, but there are other healthy behaviors that can drive fear, anxiety, or discomfort when you engage in them.

An example would include the habit of saying no. We often feel uncomfortable and self-conscious when we say no to someone, so instead we'll say yes to many things that we don't want to do and that don't match our vision for our best lives. In the long run, we feel angry and frustrated with the person asking us to do something and with ourselves for our inability to say no. But in the moment that we are asked, it's uncomfortable so we say yes and then perhaps we get overwhelmed. The better, healthier habit to develop is the habit of saying no. This frees us up to work on the things that are important to us and help us live our best lives.

Another example is creating healthy boundaries. Again, sometimes it's uncomfortable at the moment to set a healthy boundary with someone, so we let it go and then we feel frustrated because we feel we're being taken advantage of, we're not being valued for our contribution, or that unnecessary drama is coming into our lives because we don't have a boundary established. Just as with saying no, it's uncomfortable in the moment to establish a boundary yet doing so can have significant outcomes for your overall happiness.

In these situations, there is a level of immediate concern that triggers your brain, which can be experienced as feelings or voices in your head that are shouting out "Don't do it! You might die!" Your brain resists doing certain things, even if they are healthy and the right thing to do because it knows that 90% of the things that you do daily are "safe." You didn't die yesterday and you're not dead so far today so there's a good chance that continuing to do them will not kill you tomorrow. In attempting to preserve your life your biological brain causes you to resist doing new things and creating new habits, even if they are the right thing. Now, some habits will slowly kill you over time, but your brain doesn't know that. It only knows you didn't die yesterday so biologically, to keep you alive, your brain drives you to do the same behaviors and fights against you actively when you try to change. That's why change is so hard.

Interestingly, people say that they're not good at being consistent. That's not true. People are very good at being consistent. What we're not good at is changing. As I mentioned earlier, you are about 80% to 90% consistent. Much of your life is an incredible pattern of consistent behaviors. I would even say you *are* remarkably consistent. Don't listen to the voice in your head that tells you that you're not. What you're not super great at, if you're a normal human with a normal brain, is *change.* Because

your brain will actively fight against you *every time you try to change.*

    The second reason that your brain drives to habit is the amount of energy necessary to do something new. For example, think about what it is like to drive with a new driver (or remember when you were a new driver yourself). I recently drove with my latest child to get her driver's license and I'll never forget driving with her around the neighborhood. The first time she drove, I had to back the car out of the garage and down the driveway and turn it to head straight down the road, because she wasn't quite comfortable driving in reverse. I got out and moved to the passenger seat. She got in the driver's seat and her hands immediately went to the wheel in a white-knuckled death grip. She was perfectly focused. We went about 20 miles an hour around the neighborhood. Her hands never left the wheel. Her eyes never left the road. There was no distraction, no interruption. She was 100% focused on driving. I've never seen a more intentional driver, especially going 20 miles an hour around a deserted neighborhood. She turned to me in that driving experience at the end and said, "I don't know how anybody ever listens to the radio and drives at the same time. That would be so distracting."

    I laughed, and then I prayed because this is the fourth teenager I've been through this experience with, and it always goes the same way. They start out so conscientious, so focused, so disciplined, and attentive their first few times driving. But what I know is that within a couple of weeks or months, that driving experience has changed. Suddenly they're backing down the driveway with hardly even a look. They're driving down the road with the radio on and the window down and their friend in the passenger seat singing and laughing along with them. Add in the danger of texting and distraction and you wonder what possibly could have happened from her first drive around the neighborhood at 20 miles with a white-knuckled death grip on the steering wheel and where we are now, nearly a year later, driving carefree and, at times, less attentively than I would like.

The answer is *habit*. Driving has become a habit, and this is important for your brain because when something becomes a habit, it takes less energy for your brain to engage in it. The energy necessary for you to drive now is not the same energy it took the first time you drove and the energy for my daughter now is far less than the energy of her first-time driving. If you had to put the same amount of energy in every time you drove a car, you would be physically and mentally exhausted. Exerting that much energy and focus regularly is more than your brain and body can reasonably sustain. Once your brain triggers that you are repeating an action, it immediately goes into habit mode and you start doing the same consistent behavior. Now, driving doesn't require nearly the mental energy it did before because habits take significantly less mental energy. Your biological brain is designed to drive you to create and maintain habits so that you spend less of your precious energy starting from scratch every time you must do something – whether you are brushing your teeth or driving a car.

To a certain extent, your brain is stuck in a scarcity mentality related to focus and energy. From an evolutionary perspective, your brain doesn't know when your next meal is coming and therefore when it might get another boost of energy. Thousands of years ago, your ancestors went for days or weeks without food. Now thousands of years later, your modern brain persists in its ability to conserve energy. To conserve energy, all it must do is get you to do the same thing consistently over time – that's called a habit. Your brain forces you into habits because it is wired for safety, efficiency, and energy conservation. In doing the same things consistently, your brain will spend less energy on those established behaviors and will focus on new behaviors. New behaviors take energy and are perceived by the brain as dangerous; your brain doesn't like new, which explains how we have evolved into beings who spend 80% to 90% of our activity in habit mode.

That day as I sat on my nice bed in my nice house next to my beautiful wife, getting ready to go wake up my wonderful kids and drive my nice car to my good job, I knew I had to change. Intuitively, I knew that my life had not gotten to a place of darkness in a single day, and intuitively I knew I could not turn that darkness into light with a single enormous action. As I studied habits, I learned that my intuition was backed by scientific research and best practices. Much of this research goes against a very basic paradigm best summed up by the statement: "go big or go home." We live in a "go big or go home" society and in a culture that impatiently demands immediate gratification.

Often, as we look for solutions to big problems, we think that we need big solutions and further think that through those big solutions, we should see immediate results. But research and best practices in healthy habit formation show us that the way to see success in habits comes down to *small behaviors done consistently*. This is the first rule of habit: *start small*. When I tried to go big in the past, I almost always failed. I am sure you can think of a time when this was true for you as well.

Starting in the next chapter we will discuss how to use this first rule of habits, to start small, to create the daily consistent actions necessary to create lasting happiness and positive change in your life. Let's get started!

Your Happily Ever After doesn't come because you hope for it. It comes when you create your own Happily Ever Habits!

CHAPTER 6

the first key to new habits: start small

Too often our habit change is dependent on motivation. Maybe your motivation loop is similar to what I experience. I'm very motivated at 8:00 p.m. to do things. The problem is, I'm motivated to do things at 6:00 a.m.! Then 6 a.m. comes, and I feel very motivated, to do something at 8 p.m.! At the moment, at 8:00 p.m., I rarely feel like doing something. I'm sitting on my couch thinking that I know I need to work out, read or send a few positive text messages to people to brighten my day and theirs. Or I know I need to call a sibling or friend that I haven't talked with in a long time but at 8:00 p.m. I don't feel like it … and I don't feel like it two hours later at 10:00 p.m. At 10:00 p.m. I am certain I will feel like it tomorrow at 6:00 a.m., so I tell myself that I'll go to bed a bit early, get up at 5:45 a.m. tomorrow, and that by 6:00 a.m. I will feel energized and motivated to tackle the tasks I know I need to take on *now*.

It's remarkable how certain I am at 8:00 p.m. that I will be motivated at 6:00 a.m. tomorrow. What's even more astonishing is that at 6:00 a.m., completely lacking motivation, I'm certain that I will be motivated at 8:00 p.m. So, 5:45 a.m. rolls around and I think "My goodness, I don't have a lot going on today. I'm kind of tired. I'm going to sleep in. I won't push too hard through the day and by 8:00 p.m., I will feel rested and energized to tackle the task." That death loop of (lack of) motivation happens day after day as at 8:00 p.m. I convince myself I'll feel motivated at 6:00 a.m. and then at 6:00 a.m. I convince myself that I'll be motivated at 8:00 p.m. Around and around we go. Maybe you've done the same thing.

The underlying cause of procrastination is that you are relying on motivation, your belief that at some unique time in the future, you will feel a burst of motivation to accomplish a task. But that moment of motivation is not right now, because right now I don't feel like it. The way to combat that problem is to start small.

For example, I have created a habit of doing 100 pushups a day. When I first decided to do this, I could do exactly five pushups at a time. There's no chance I could do 100 standard pushups that day, but I could do five. So, my first habit to ensure I would not fail was to do five pushups consistently at one time. *Your first habit goal is not to see results. Your first habit goal is to build consistency.* When I started with five pushups, I didn't suddenly see muscles bulging out of my shirt. What I did do is start a pattern at a specific time and place with a specific mental attitude toward doing pushups.

> *On starting small:*
>
> *"... I have 30 minutes a day between working full-time, kids at school, making dinner, volunteering. I have 30 minutes I'm going to choose because I want something different for my future ... I'm not gonna watch that Netflix for 30 minutes. Instead, I'm gonna put it towards the person I want to become. And that made it easier for me. I was like, this is that lifestyle that I want and so I'm gonna take that 30 minutes today.*
>
> *I could see 30 minutes or 30 seconds of progress. 30 seconds and I really had to celebrate that I am 30 seconds closer to the workout, the body, the health, the lifestyle that I want to be in my business. I am 30 minutes closer [to] that big project. That's still going to take me two hours, but I'm 30 minutes into it. And now I'm feeling like, 'Okay, Megan, you're doing this.'"*
>
> *— Megan Pyrah, from the Happily Ever Habits podcast*

I didn't have to rely on a huge burst of motivation because no matter how unmotivated I was at either 6:00 a.m. or 8:00 p.m. I could muster enough motivation to get down and do five or six pushups. Suddenly I was doing 10 pushups and then I was doing 20 pushups and finally, I was doing 100 pushups a day. But the first rule was to start small and the first goal was to build consistency.

Hopefully, by now, you have connected with both the practical and emotional reasoning behind starting your habits small. I encourage you to not allow yourself to slip into the downward pattern but to create positive movement in your life, where you can go from darkness to a little bit lighter every. Just as I did when I was sitting on my nice bed in my nice house next to my beautiful wife, I hope you decide today can be just a little bit lighter than yesterday. We don't have to wish for some grand

On deciding to be better today than you were yesterday:

"Results create belief. In the beginning when we're trying to do something, it's difficult to have any belief at all that we can do it well, only because we have ... no reference point, really. I think that the key part in the early, early beginning is taking action and trying to get some of those early results ... Let's use a simple example of working out. [It's a] very cliche example, but it works.

"So, working out, you're not going to see your body change in the first week, but maybe you were like, "Oh, I couldn't even do 10 pushups before, but now I can do 15." Hey, that's a win. Those little things start to compound and raise your belief and learning to celebrate those little wins."

Eric Chow, from the Happily Ever Habits podcast

manifestation from heaven to suddenly pour light into our lives. We can make small, incremental improvements to be a little bit better today and be proud of that. Then, we will repeat that, consciously attempting to be a little bit better tomorrow, and to be proud of that, too. We can choose to push through when we face an obstacle because we know we can do the small things necessary to build consistency, momentum, and a positive direction by starting small and being consistent.

Whatever you choose as your daily action, my suggestion is to make it small. A good rule of thumb is James Clear's two-minute rule. You should be able to complete the habit in two minutes or less. If it takes longer than that, you may need to rely on motivation, which as we all know is unpredictable. Right now, you just want to build consistency and momentum because consistency will beat motivation every time.

MASTERMIND ASSIGNMENT

Take a few minutes now and in the space on the next page write down each of the core values that you identified in the last chapter, and for each value identify a single daily action you can take that can be completed in two minutes or less. And together we will start your journey toward being a little bit lighter and happier tomorrow than you are today.

Scan this QR code for a
video walkthrough of
the
Choose Your Habit
Action Activity

HABIT PLAN

CORE VALUE	DAILY ACTION	WHEN TO COMPLETE

The most significant benefit to starting small is psychological. Imagine the following two scenarios. In scenario one you set a goal to exercise for 30 minutes every morning. But you wake up and you're late, you're rushed and you quickly get ready for work. You speed out the door to work and the entire day you are stressed about and emotionally brought down by the fact that you didn't get your exercise in this morning. You feel like a failure on day one. You come home, thinking you will exercise today and then your daughter reminds you that she has a softball game, so you go. The whole time you're stressed, and you still feel like a failure because you haven't exercised for 30 minutes. You get home at 8:00 p.m. and you know you need to work out for 30 minutes, but you have had a long day and the motivation necessary just isn't there now. You feel defeated. Now you start thinking about why you even tried to implement a new habit. You'll never consistently exercise and change your health habits. So why even try tomorrow when you are sure tomorrow will be just as difficult as today? This starts a psychological downward spiral and the likelihood of you now staying positive and consistent with a 30-minute exercise habit is almost dead before you even start.

Consider an alternate scenario. In scenario two, you set an intention to do 10 air squats, 10 sit-ups, and 10 pushups to start your new healthy habit. Every day you wake up and you're still late and feeling rushed, but you know it only takes five minutes to do your 10 air squats, 10 sit-ups, and 10 pushups. Although your form is not great and a trainer might tell you to slow down to get the full impact of the exercise, you bust out your 10, 10, and 10. You celebrate the fact that you have gotten in your exercise even on a morning when you hit the snooze button a couple of times. As you go through your day, you now have the confidence and the momentum of having completed a difficult task, even in the face of the opposition created by your biological brain that doesn't want you to do new things. This helps you in other tasks as you build confidence

and feel the energy and drive of having accomplished your new habit.

You come home from work and face the same scenario. You need to take your daughter to her softball game. As you sit and cheer for her, you're present because you're not worried about what you haven't done yet today. You are proud of what you did accomplish. You come home and it's 8:00 p.m. and you feel confident that tomorrow morning you can get up and do it again. You eat a slightly healthier dinner because you're not defeated. You don't feel down on yourself. You don't feel like you could never accomplish this. You feel powerful and positive, and you feel the momentum of having completed your new habit, even though it was only 10 air squats, 10 sit-ups, and 10 pushups.

What happens the next morning? You come into the morning with that powerful momentum and optimism. And once again you do your three 10s and go through a similar day. The next day may even be the same thing. What happens over time is you do the 10 pushups and think "I've got more in me." So, you do 20 pushups then you do the 10 air squats and think "I can do more." So, you do more. You don't have to do more every day because your first habit goal is just to build consistency rather than to see results. Some days you push a little further and soon every single morning you're consistently getting in your 10, 10, 10. Now you decide to stretch that habit and add some cardio. Nothing huge, just 10 minutes of cardio every morning. You add it with confidence because you have had a positive experience of small habits done consistently over time, The first goal is to simply build momentum and consistency which leads to having powerful habit experiences that drive you to do more successful behaviors day after day.

You can achieve your first habit goal today! The key is to establish a consistent pattern of behavior, without focusing on immediate results. Begin with small steps to boost your consistency. This initial action will set you in motion and create momentum. But remember, we still have more to do! Starting small is merely the first of three essential habit steps required for consistency and success as you start and stick with the habits that will create your happily ever habits.

Your Happily Ever After doesn't come because you hope for it. It comes when you create your own Happily Ever Habits!

CHAPTER 7

the second key to new habits: make it easy

The next key to implementing habits after starting small is to make the habit as easy as possible. This aspect of habit creation is connected to *intention*. Making things small relates to motivation because the mistake we often make is to try to "go big or go home" and expect that we will have large bursts of motivation consistently, which simply is not true. We start small so that even when we don't feel motivated, we can still build momentum and make improvements by building consistency through small steps. Making the habit easy deals with *intention* because intention is as unreliable as motivation. We overcome the intention gap by making things as easy as possible.

Think of all the things you have intended to do in your life and have not done. Think of the things you intend to do now every day but simply don't. It's not because you are remarkably deficient or incredibly inept. You don't do them because you are a human being and as human beings, we set intentions and then try to match our actions to those intentions. We are not particularly good at doing this, either because (1) we don't accurately account for the amount of time necessary to complete those actions; (2) we don't account for the amount of motivation necessary to accomplish those actions; or (3) we don't account for outside influences that prevent us from accomplishing those actions. We may intend to do 10 things but, in reality, we only have time to do seven, or we intend to do 10 things and our motivation to do all 10 fails after the first two or three, or we intend to do 10 things unaware that there will be five crises we will be forced to deal with today. It's also possible that we will allow ourselves to be distracted by five unimportant things that sap our time and energy.

We constantly face the battle between what we intend to do and what we actually do. Nowhere is this truer than in creating our habits. We intend to eat better but we don't. We intend to save more money, but we don't. We intend to be charitable and kind, we intend to read more, we intend to contribute significantly to the lives of others. But for one reason or another, there is always a gap between what we intend and what we execute regardless of whether the habit that we're focusing on is related to our health, wealth, self-improvement, or something else. To close that gap and get us closer to what we intend to do, be or become and the life we intend to have, we need to strive to make our habits as easy as possible. This will help us overcome the *intention gap.*

Habit stacking

There are three specific methods you can use to make a habit easier. The first is one that James Clear calls *habit stacking,* which is based on the work of Charles Duhigg in his book *The Power of Habits* and involves utilizing habit cues. The idea is to take a habit you are already doing and partner it with a habit that you want to start doing.

Let me tell you a story that illustrates how this worked in my life. For a long time, I wanted to make my mornings better. I had read many articles, I'd listened to podcasts, was a part of groups, and had read in multiple books that the way you start your morning impacts your mood and outlook for the rest of the day. I talked about this exclusively in chapter two because it is so important. When I began my journey toward healthy habits in my efforts to have a happier life, gratitude journaling was one of the habits that I wanted to incorporate. It kept floating into my mind as I was floating into the darkness. But it was not just gratitude journaling I was interested in, I needed to start with a solid morning plan. When I finally decided it was time to start crawling toward the light, I knew that one of the biggest challenges I faced was my own mental patterns.

The way I thought, and the way that I was seeing the world had to change. I had to change the setting of my sails. As I mentioned in chapter two, starting my morning off right is one way to do that because it sets your sails for the rest of the day.

For me, habit stacking is what helped me break through all the issues I had experienced in previous attempts at having successful mornings. I'd tried getting up early, doing great morning routines, and exercising consistently. In fact, I'd tried many different morning plans and routines that simply hadn't worked. I could never have a consistent, positive morning experience – until I started habit stacking. Here's how it worked for me, and this story shows you the clues of how it can work for you.

During the COVID-19 lockdown, as everybody got bored at home, we decided it was time to get a dog. My wife found a little Shorkie she wanted. In the middle of the lockdown, we added a dog to the mix! Like thousands of other families, my children reassured me that they were going to help take care of the dog. But just like you and I, there's a gap between what they *said they would do* and what they actually *did*.

As soon as we got the dog, their offers to help became non-existent. The most significant help that is required is getting up at 5:30 every morning to let the dog out of her crate to go outside. This responsibility immediately fell solely on me. Initially, I was a bit frustrated with eight or nine people living in the house. Why did I have to bear the full brunt of that responsibility?

This became a point of frustration, but I didn't want to sink into anger and despair. I had enough of that in my life without getting mad about having to let a dog out. Instead, I decided to use habit stacking as a way to implement the positive morning routine. I'd been trying to start for years. So, every morning at 5:30 I would get up, open the crate door, pick up the dog, set her outside to do her morning business, and immediately turn around, sit down, and start writing down three things that I was grateful for. That's the first habit stack: taking something you are already doing and tying a new behavior to it.

I was already getting up at 5:30 every morning to let the dog out, so I decided to let that become the trigger of the new habit I wanted. From there, I added additional important morning habits. After writing in my gratitude journal, I would drink 10-12 ounces of water because that has a positive impact on your mental, emotional, and physical health. From there, added 10 minutes of exercise just to get my body moving; yoga, stretching, a quick exercise routine, or even just going for a 10-minute walk or jog would do the trick.

From there, I would hop into a cold shower and my positive morning was off and running. I had already addressed my mental state through gratitude journaling. I had improved my physical state through drinking water and movement and a cold shower, and now I was ready, and in a much more positive frame of mind, to face the day.

Another habit stack that I used in a totally different way was flossing my teeth. I would consistently have embarrassing visits to the dentist because I could never get consistent in flossing. And then I decided to habit stack. I took some flossers and put them in my car. Every day when I drive to work, the first red light I hit is my habit-stacking trigger. I grab a flosser from the center console of my car and quickly floss my teeth while waiting for the red light to change. Now, the people in the car next to me might be a little grossed out by my habit, but I don't really care because it makes it so much easier every time I visit the dentist.

The habit-stacking process is simple. Look at your existing routines. You already have a morning routine. It likely includes taking a shower, getting dressed, and brushing your teeth. These are three powerful options for a habit stack. Think through what specific action you will take immediately after brushing your teeth, immediately after taking a shower, or immediately after getting dressed. If you work from home, you have a start-your-day routine. You sit down, you turn on your laptop. And maybe the first thing you do is check your email. That can be a powerful time to habit stack. You might even stack ahead of checking your email. Before checking my email, I will _____. After checking my email, I will always _____. Right before eating lunch, I will always _____. There are dozens of other actions that you already take every day, how can you stack another small habit with the ones you already have?

This is an example of making a habit easier by identifying patterns you already engage in. For me, that was stopping at an inevitable red light while driving to work. This is the easiest part because you are already engaged in dozens of consistent habits every day. From your morning routine to your work routine to your bedtime routine – everything you currently do has a consistent set of behaviors attached to it. To make new habit formation easier, simply identify the new behavior you want to incorporate into your routine and which existing behavior you are going to stack with the new habit.

MASTERMIND ASSIGNMENT

Create a habit stacking commitment using the table below, or journal about it and post your commitments in your planner or calendar. Over time, you can stack several new habits on top of the action you are already taking.

Scan this QR code for a video walkthrough of the
Create Your Habit Stack Activity

HABIT STACK

WHEN I (CURRENT ACTION):	
AT (TIME AND LOCATION):	
I WILL (NEW ACTION):	

Change your environment

Another way to make forming new habits easier is to change your environment. Our lives are dominated by our environment. If I came to your house, I could tell a lot about you just by looking around. If I opened your fridge or your pantry, I'd be able to tell what foods you eat. If I looked in your closet, I could learn what kind of clothes you wear. If I looked in your living room, I could tell you whether television, books, or hobbies are more important to you simply based on where the TV and remote are located and what objects are in the room. If I opened your phone and looked at your home screen, I could easily tell what things are most important to you, because things that are most important to us take a prominent place in our environment.

When you want to create a new habit, making even small changes to your environment is a powerful tool. In both of my habit-stacking stories (keeping a gratitude journal and flossing my teeth), changes to my environment were keys to my success. I created the environment I needed to keep a gratitude journal by putting my journal on the table next to the back door every night. If that journal were hidden away in a drawer on my nightstand, what would happen if I forgot it when I let the dog out in the morning? I would have to leave the dog outside and creep back into the bedroom (without waking up my wife), open the drawer, grab my gratitude journal, and then search through the kitchen for a pen or pencil. That's far too many steps and something that needs to be easy is now incredibly complicated, which means the likelihood of me writing in my journal goes way down. Occasionally, if I feel motivated, I might go through the process of retrieving the journal and a pen, but *I don't want to rely on motivation. I want to rely on easy and small habits that build to generate consistency and positive momentum.*

With this in mind, I crafted my morning environment to support exactly what I needed to do: let the dog out, turn around, take one step, sit down, and write in my journal. Of course,iIt did require the implementation of the habit, including my nightly routine of grabbing my journal from my work desk and putting it next to the door where the dog goes out. But I always make sure after writing in my gratitude journal that it goes on my work desk. Worst case scenario, if I forget to put it on the kitchen table, I can let the dog out and then head to my desk to grab it because one of the first things I do each morning is to start my day at my desk and my journal is right there. Even if I forget to leave it by the back door, I can quickly grab it from my desk and write my gratitude list before I even turn on my computer. My environment is specifically organized to make it easier for me to sustain this habit. It's *intentional.* My flossing habit is similar. Buying easy-to-use flossers and putting them in the center console of my car makes it far more likely that when I stop at a red light, I'll remember to open the center console and grab one. If those flossers weren't there, the likelihood of me flossing drops dramatically.

You can do the same thing with any habit you want to implement simply by changing your environment to support it. If you want to read more, put your book in a prominent place on your work desk or on the table right next to the couch. Then when you sit down, instead of reaching for the TV remote or your phone you might reach for your book instead.

If you want to exercise more, put exercise equipment, your running shoes, or workout clothes in a more prominent place. As I mentioned earlier, I try to do 100 pushups a day, so I have pushup bars right next to my work desk. This makes it much easier for me to do 25 pushups at a time. I try to do that four times a day to get in my 100 pushups. When you want to make it easier to successfully implement a habit, crafting an environment to support your new habit will be the most important factor in your success. ***Change your environment and it will be significantly easier for you to implement your habit.***

Habit tracking

The third method to make habits easier is to use tracking. ***When we track something, it becomes far easier to be consistent because tracking drives awareness.*** As we learned earlier, most of our habits are done subconsciously to save energy, which means we have no conscious awareness of them. As soon as we track something, we become aware, and that awareness leads to behavior changes. Health experts will tell you that the easiest way to eat less is to track what you eat because your subconscious eating becomes conscious as soon as you start putting every calorie into your food tracker.

It is the same with your finances. If you want to be better at managing your finances, the first habit will be tracking your finances. Personal finance gurus will always encourage you to download their free budget tracker, where you assign a certain amount of money to every budget item and then consciously track how much money you spend on each category like charitable contributions, car and mortgage payments, utilities, groceries, and eating out. If you give yourself a certain amount of money every month and then track how much money you spend, you become far more aware of your expenditures. That awareness can help you change your behavior.

Tracking works for any habit you want to implement. In my free "Happily Ever Habit Guide," available on my website (www.thejasonharwood.com) you will find a habit track where you simply write down the habit that you want to implement and check off every day you complete it. There is also a column for celebrating every time you complete your habit. More about that later!

Every Monday morning, one of the first things I do is print off my tracker for the week. I identify the key behaviors that I want to engage in daily for that week. I keep my tracker in a conspicuous place, which is another way of saying I manipulate my environment to assist my habits so that when I have a couple of extra minutes, instead of watching YouTube or scrolling TikTok, I see my habit sheet and identify a habit that I want to work on that day such as doing my 25 pushups. Because I'm tracking pushups as a daily habit, I'm far more likely to do 25 pushups rather than waste five minutes scrolling. Implementing my habits becomes easier because I'm tracking, and tracking creates awareness. In that process, I'm playing a game with my mind as I see how many days in a row I can do a new action or behavior.

WEEKLY HABIT TRACKER

HABIT:

HABIT:

HABIT:

You can make it a game for yourself to see how many days in a row you can perform a certain activity. Once you've identified a behavior that you want to engage in, your brain will work to help you remember to do that thing and then it becomes easier. As you move into full awareness of your behaviors through tracking, completion of that task becomes easier.

We all have a gap between what we intend to do and what we actually do. Often that gap is full of good intentions that are met with challenges. Not completing a task or habit could happen for many reasons. It could be that it is too difficult, or we don't have enough time. Maybe we overestimated our ability, which can happen when we are doing something new. The good news is that you can shrink that intention gap and come closer to where you want to be by making small changes using these three methods: stacking, changing your environment, and tracking. Your habits are likely to develop more easily, and your consistency will increase dramatically. When your consistency increases dramatically, your results will follow.

So far, we've talked about how to start small so you can overcome the *motivation challenge*. We've talked about making new habits easier through stacking, environmental changes, and tracking to help you overcome the *intention challenge*. The last tool to use to solidify your new habit is to celebrate small wins, which are primarily intended to overcome the *enthusiasm challenge*.

MASTERMIND ASSIGNMENT

Have you determined how you are going to stack your habits using the box on page 57? Now, I challenge you to use a tracker to track your identified habits for a week, treating it as a game to see how many days in a row you can consistently complete your new habit. To get a FREE copy of my tracker, go to www.thejasonharwood.com or use the QR code below to download the *Happily Ever Habits Guide*. For now, use the space below to create a short list of the daily, weekly, and monthly habits you want to track. Remember, keep it simple to start!

Scan this QR code to
get your
Happily Habits Guide!

Scan this QR code for a
video walkthrough of
the
Track Your Habits
Activity

Your Happily Ever After doesn't come because you hope for it. It comes when you create your own Happily Ever Habits!

CHAPTER 8

the third key to new habits: celebrate small wins

Before we talk about celebrating small wins and why it's important, let's about preferences. We attribute positive or negative feelings toward people, things, and situations. We prefer certain things over others and a lot of the time we don't even know why. We just know that we feel enthusiastic about certain things and completely lack enthusiasm about others. For example, I grew up in Utah, so I loved the Utah Jazz for basketball but also loved the NY Mets Major League Baseball team and the Chicago Bears NFL team. I probably loved these teams because my older brother loved them. Over time, I developed a preference for these teams and really enjoyed the camaraderie of celebrating their successes with other fans. I probably would have had a better time rooting for more winning teams, but it doesn't matter – I prefer the Mets and the Bears.

Preferences can go a little deeper than liking something or being enthusiastic about it. If you observe your own thoughts and preferences, you may find, like I do, that you take it a bit further and assign labels of "good" or "bad" to people, places, things, and situations. These are part of your core beliefs. For example, the fact that I am enthusiastic about the Mets and the Bears is supported by my core belief that they are great teams. These are not intentional core beliefs, and I am unaware of exactly when those beliefs formed.

It's important to know that you have core beliefs and preferences that influence habits and that those core beliefs, like your automatic routines, may be running in the background without your awareness. They are unintentional. You may be predisposed to not liking certain foods, like broccoli. You know it's good for you, but you prefer cucumbers. Someone else may love broccoli and hate cucumbers. It's a matter of preference – but both vegetables are good for you.

You think of broccoli or cucumbers as "bad," just as you might think of other things that are technically good for you as "bad." This tendency to attribute "goodness" or "badness" to activities and situations *does* play a very significant role in our happiness and in the habits, we choose to embrace. We can overcome this attribution of "good" or "bad" by celebrating small wins because there are certain habits that you've already built a mental barrier against – maybe it's exercise, maybe it's saving some of your money, maybe it's eating certain foods, writing in a journal, or reading books. And when those things are suggested, you immediately think to yourself: "Ooh, that's bad" or "Ooh, that's good." Many of the things that you identify as good you're already doing. Likewise, many of the things that you identify as bad you aren't doing.

The real challenges are when a potential habit you've identified in your mind as bad is a habit that would make you happier, healthier, a better manager of your money or bring you closer to aligning with your core values. You already have some of these in your mind – the things that you know you should be doing but aren't (like reading or writing in a journal daily), or the things that you know you shouldn't be doing but you are (like scrolling on TikTok)

Most of us would agree there are valuable mental, physical, and emotional benefits of doing yoga. Yet, I bet most of us don't do yoga.

Why do we refuse to do things we know are good for us and continue to do things that we know are bad? How can we overcome this? One way we can overcome this is through *celebrating small wins*. When you celebrate small wins, you trick your mind and turn a negative core belief about a habit you deep down don't want to do (like reading more or doing yoga or meditating, for example) into a positive one. Celebrating small wins changes your mental programming related to your attitudes toward those behaviors. So, you read more each day or do 10 minutes of yoga or practice a deliberate act of kindness and then you celebrate every time you do it. As you build a small and easy habit, you drive it deeper into your mind by celebrating its completion every time. You significantly reduce the amount of time necessary to implement it as a consistent habit and you solidify the likelihood of maintaining consistency this way. As we discussed earlier, this is mostly based on the biology of your brain. When you complete your new behavior be sure to celebrate in a small way like giving yourself a high five or patting yourself on the back. *Literally* – pat yourself on the back.

On celebrating your achievements:

"... you really don't want to wait till you reach your goal to celebrate the wins. I want you and really encourage you to notice and celebrate all the learning, all the growth along the way. So, for example, in this situation [where] you weren't doing your goal, you didn't get it done for a week, but you learned that you don't really want to do it at 5:00 a.m.

Or the growth is you decided you're going to go to bed earlier; even though you haven't been necessarily reaching that goal every day that you want to, celebrate that learning and celebrate that goal [and] the growth ... along the way towards your goal."

– Ceri Payne, from the Happily Ever Habits podcast

My go-to celebration is a single- or double-fisted flex. You can do a fist bump and give yourself a "Yes!" You can pump a fist in the air and tell yourself "Nice job." These small celebrations do something interesting in your brain. They release dopamine, the "feel good" chemical. When you do something that you enjoy, dopamine is released which tells your brain that the activity you are doing is enjoyable. This drives the idea deep into your brain that you should do that activity or habit again. People who run often experience this type of chemical release; it's called a "runner's high." This "runner's high" happens when you've gotten through the initial pain and discomfort of running and the "feel good" chemicals in your brain like dopamine are released and your body is pumping and suddenly you feel really good. You have started to override some of the pain and discomfort through brain chemistry and biology. You can do the same thing with habit creation by celebrating small wins.

When I started my habit of doing a hundred pushups, I knew that I would not be able to do a hundred straight pushups to start. I still can't, but I can do four sets of 25. And in fact, I broke it down even further, where I would do a set of 10, then celebrate, then a set of 10 and celebrate, and then five more pushups and celebrate. I would celebrate small victories between sets. I would fist pump. I would hit myself on the chest. I would give myself a flex and tell myself, "Nice job. You're doing great." Suddenly, something that had previously been unattractive became a behavior that I looked forward to doing and my brain encouraged me because my brain was wired to understand that once I did the behavior, it would get the dopamine hit that it craved when I celebrated my small success.

Celebrating small wins is not a difficult or challenging thing to do. But we fail to celebrate our small successes because we think we'll look silly or because we don't think that the behavior that we are engaging in is worth celebrating. We condition ourselves to think we must do something huge or have a major, significant accomplishment before we can celebrate. Remember, we live in a "go big or go home" culture where small things don't matter – only doing huge, nearly impossible things are worthy of celebrating. We also believe if we celebrate small things along the way, it's petty and insignificant. After all, who do we think we are for celebrating five pushups? This cultural issue doesn't support positive behavior change. As you establish your new habits and actions to support them, you're going to have to fight against your brain.

The first thing you will need to fight against is something we have already talked about: your brain's desire to conserve energy by staying in automatic mode. By now you know that your brain doesn't want you to engage in new behaviors because it knows that if you do the same things you've always done, you're going to stay alive. Anytime you introduce something new, you run the risk of doing something that might kill you and your brain doesn't want to take that chance so it's going to try to fight to keep you locked into your existing pattern. Be prepared to face this roadblock.

Secondly, your brain will not want to expend the energy necessary to learn and incorporate new things. Doing new things is difficult because your brain would rather that you continue to do the same things you've always done. After all, that's easier. When you take less brain power, you use less energy. Your brain wants to make sure you have conserved enough energy in case there's a crisis.

The third roadblock is societal. I alluded to it earlier when I talked about our "go big or go home" culture. We don't celebrate small things because, to us as a society, small things are no big deal. We feel that celebrating something like 25 pushups is silly, ineffective, or we don't deserve it. We also believe it's okay to celebrate others but celebrating ourselves is boastful. You may have your own preconceived notions about your value and the value of celebrating your successes as a way to help make your new habits stick. Be prepared for that challenge. You can try to implement habits without celebrating. You will be successful if you keep them small, make them easy, change your environment, track them, and implement some of the other methods and techniques that I have described.

But keep in mind that you will implement a new habit faster if you also consider the biology and chemistry of your brain and understand that *when you celebrate small wins you get that important dopamine hit that drives the new habit into your brain faster*. This allows you to assimilate the new behavior more quickly. So, celebrate every time you accomplish that new habit!

You may have heard that it takes 21 days to develop a habit. That's not entirely accurate. At around 21 days it's as easy as it's ever going to be, but it only takes a couple of days to start a new habit. On the flip side, it only takes a couple of days to *stop* a habit. As soon as you do something two or three days in a row, it's a habit. As soon as you don't do it two or three days in a row that's a new habit of not doing the behavior. When you celebrate, you increase the likelihood that your new habit will take hold because you increase the connection between your brain and that activity. *When you strengthen the bond of the habit in your brain through celebration, your ability to implement and stick with the new habit increases dramatically.*

MASTERMIND ASSIGNMENT

Determine how you will celebrate when you complete a new action. Create a celebration plan for every habit or action you are adding to your daily or weekly routine.

HABIT CELEBRATION

COMPLETED ACTION	HOW I WILL CELEBRATE (FIST PUMP, HAPPY DANCE, "YES!")

Build a circle

The last tool to consider in developing habits is to build a circle of friends who will help you achieve your habits. There's a difference between friends and accomplices. Friends are those who help you achieve your best and accomplices are those who help you maintain the status quo (or try to help you achieve the worst that you can become). When you tell somebody about a new habit that you're hoping to implement, a new idea of how you can become a better person, or a core character trait that you want to develop, their response is a great indicator of whether they are a friend or an accomplice. Are they trying to help you become the very best version of yourself or are they trying to keep you in the status quo? This is a real challenge because for some people *your* status quo has a direct impact on *their* status quo. Sometimes if you start making dramatic changes in your life, it requires other people to make dramatic changes, too, and not everybody is ready to make dramatic changes at the same time.

True friends will see your desire for improvement; not just the desire to have more but the desire to be better and to have a happier life full of meaning and purpose. They will get excited about the things you're excited about and will be passionate about the things that you want to invest in. They will be supportive of your efforts.

When you talk about small, easy, and celebrating, one good experiment is to think of the person to whom you would text your best celebration GIF. Imagine you've been working on your habit for a week. You've done five air squats and five modified pushups every single morning. And you send a GIF to somebody to celebrate your wins. Start thinking now about whom you would send that to and who would respond with their best celebration GIF.

It's impossible to share sample GIFs in a book! If you go to thejasonharwood.com or use the QR code below, you can download GIFs you can use to create your own customized celebrations.

Scan this QR code for a video walkthrough of the

<u>Celebrate Small Wins Activity</u>

<u>On why we need other people to help us succeed:</u>

"Another thing that I think helps me when I get into those dark places is that, and, and we all do this ... we go inside, you know, "Oh, woe is me." Things are terrible on [the] outside. The best way to stop that is to get outside yourself is to find somebody else that you can help, find somebody else that you serve, because then the focus is off you and on somebody else. And you have this attitude of, "Hey, I'm helping this person. My life is having meaning to somebody else."

I think that's what it's all about. You know ... our life should be about service, whether you believe in God, whether serving your God, but certainly serving your fellow man in whatever capacity you can do that. I think that's something that I guess I was fortunate enough to learn as I was going through team sports. And I mean, we're all part of a team in some way, whether it's our family or our church or business or whatever it is. So, I guess I would ... use that theme of, "Hey, be part of something that's bigger than yourself."

Terry Tucker, from the Happily Ever Habits podcast

Also think about who would criticize you and say, "You only did five pushups a day and they were modified. I don't see any results." Don't include these people because what you are trying to create is a celebration circle, not a negativity circle. There is power in surrounding yourself with those who will celebrate along with you. I learned this principle as a Boy Scout. We did a fair amount of camping and I learned early on that one of the first steps to extinguish the fire is to start spreading out all the embers and half-burned logs from the fire. You separate them from each other as far as you can within the fire ring. If the embers stay close together, they'll burn for a long time. That's what you want in your celebration circle. When embers and logs are separated on their own, the fire will go out quickly. That's what you don't want in a celebration circle because the first step to extinguishing your habit is to separate yourself from those who could encourage you along your new path.

When we celebrate together, it brings more excitement. Think about why people go to live sporting events. You can watch the sporting event at home, but to be in the stadium with a bunch of other people who are as wild and crazy about your team as you make it so much more meaningful and engaging. When your team scores, you stand up and yell and scream and high five and cheer right along with them.

During a Major League baseball game, you sing right along with them at the seventh-inning stretch. You are with a bunch of people who are passionate about the same things you're passionate about. That's your celebration circle. You can build the same thing in your life – your very own celebration circle, your very own group of people who will cheer you on when you do great things.

On the need for cheerleaders in our new habits:

"The opposite of grieving and loss is connection. So, one of the habits that we need to do in order for us to be happy again is that we need to connect on a regular basis with people. That's how we are gonna be happy and healthy.

People are going to help us when we are not at our best spot in life, or when we're struggling. We just link arms with them and they'll carry us through. So that was the habit that we begin to incorporate on a consistent basis: Connections with happy people."

—Jason Clawson, from the Happily Ever Habits podcast

A second reason to have a group of people around you is accountability. The first person that we lie to or make an excuse to is ourselves. If you're like me, you're very good at listening to and accepting your own lies. The next person that you would have to lie to is very important. If you have somebody else that you will have to check in with or recount your day to, it will become more difficult to skip your key behaviors because you won't be as willing to let others down. We will go to great lengths not to let down a friend or family member even though we will often let ourselves down quickly. Having someone who will lovingly check in on you is a powerful resource. I chose those words carefully: "lovingly check in on you." This is a unique skill set and I have found it is not often successfully done by a spouse. You might need to choose someone else to be your accountability partner. Someone who, when you express a setback or a failure, will show you the proper level of grace and acceptance while still holding you to your commitment because they know you may have taken a step back but are not ready to sit down. Sometimes people very close to us will allow us to both step back and sit down. They may not have even been fully supportive of your new habits in the first place; this sometimes happens because a change in your habits dramatically impacts them. But when someone allows you to take a step back without allowing or encouraging you to sit down, that's a crucial member of your celebration circle. That's the person who will say, "Hey, we all mess up. Hey, we all miss a day. Hey, we all come up a little bit short sometimes, and that's okay, but we're not losing sight of the main goal. And the only way is forward." That's the person who will embrace you and acknowledge your human imperfections while still holding you true to your goals, dreams, and aspirations. Make sure the person who says to you, "Hey, it's okay. We all mess up occasionally," isn't also saying to you, "Hey, don't try again tomorrow." Or "Hey, maybe this isn't your thing," or, "Hey, I didn't really think you'd be able to pull this off anyway.".

When you have a setback, notice the way someone responds and identify whether they are a good member of your celebration circle. You need some people who will simply just celebrate with you, who will just send you the celebration GIF. You also need a couple of those people who, when you slip up, you text them and say, "Man, I missed my workout yesterday, but I promise I won't miss tomorrow." And they'll respond and say, "Hey, I've missed a workout or two as well, but tomorrow's workout is the most important. I'll be there for you." You need accountability partners who will say, "Hey, it's okay if you missed one day of your habit. Let's not miss two."

If you have a positive and supportive group around you, you are miles ahead in your habit success. If you have even one positive person around you, it will make a significant difference. The invitation for this chapter is to find a celebration circle to share your habits with and start having meaningful conversations about your new habits. As you make progress and experience setbacks, it's best if you have two to three people in your celebration circle, but at least start with one. Reach out to them today. Let them know you're studying habits. Possibly encourage them to get their own copy of this book so you can work on your habits together. If you want to be a part of a positive, encouraging habit community follow me on Instagram @thejasonharwood and join the Happier Habits Circle Group on Facebook. This is the best place to share your habit progress, successes, setbacks, and failures and get ongoing support from positive people who are pursuing similar goals.

MASTERMIND ASSIGNMENT

Using the space below, list the people in your celebration circle and how you will connect with them.

CELEBRATION CIRCLE

NAME	HOW I WILL CONTACT THEM TO CELEBRATE

Your Happily Ever After doesn't come because you hope for it. It comes when you create your own Happily Ever Habits!

CHAPTER 9

making a habit of creating new habits

Let's look at the assignments you should have completed so far, the work that you can continue to do, and the next steps to take to solidify your new habits.

We started by looking at the core character traits that are most important to you. In that chapter, you should have identified a few character traits that are critical to living a fulfilled life. Then, we took those core character traits and identified the smallest behaviors or habits you could engage in to build consistent new habits in that character trait so that it becomes a daily part of your life.

Then we looked at the three keys to creating habits: start small, make it easy, and celebrate small wins.

We learned how to make establishing habits easier by using tools such as habit stacking, changing your environment, tracking your behavior, and celebrating every small win. Remember, you should be celebrating a habit success every day, if not multiple times throughout the day. Finally, make sure you are making intentional connections to your celebration circle as well as connecting with the online community in the Happily Ever Habits circle on Facebook.

In my experience working with dozens of people on their habits, a few things are almost certain to happen from here. One is that you will still not be quite as consistent with your habits as you'd like to be. They'll be small, they'll be easy, you'll be ready to celebrate, and yet at times, you will still slip up. When you slip up, here are the steps to take to maintain your own mental momentum.

First, give yourself grace. ***Habits are not a path to perfection and your personal development will never follow a perfect path.*** When you make a mistake, acknowledge it, and give yourself space and grace for your own human nature.

The second thing to do is to fully commit back to the habit as soon as possible. We often talk about how many days it takes to make a habit. As discussed earlier in the book, popular opinion holds that it takes 21 days to make a habit. The problem with this approach is that it can really take as few as two days to create a new pattern or a new habit but if you skip a new habit twice you've now created another new pattern of *not* doing the habit. Missing once is a time for space, grace, and recommitment. Miss once, and immediately and fully commit to never missing twice.

Great habit creators are not perfect, but the best habit creators are unwilling to compromise what's most important to them. If you have identified a behavior as important to you, one of the issues will be trying to talk yourself out of it later. You'll slip up once and give yourself space and grace. Then in the moment of needing to recommit, you might be tempted to readjust your expectations of yourself. You might be tempted to think that you're fine and that you don't really need to put in the effort to grow; that you don't really need to work intentionally to be a little happier every day and you don't really need to put in the work required for positive habit creation. In that moment there is the temptation to doubt that you can make the changes that will actually build to greatness over time.

As you begin to doubt, you will start to readjust your life back to the way it was before you started your positive habit journey. This is the moment that you must commit and say you are never going back. Instead, you are committed to moving forward no matter how small the steps are. Even if you occasionally miss, commit to making consistent, positive momentum upward toward the light of happiness. Don't fall into the trap of pretending that the way things have always been is the way you want things to always be. You started this habit journey for a reason. You felt compelled to make changes for a reason, and when it gets difficult, you will have to combat the temptation to convince yourself that your old ways of being are good enough.

Very quickly, you'll start to see progress, growth, and improvement. You'll start to feel better. You'll start to have the light of joy shining back in your life. The temptation at this point is to think you've arrived and that you can stop doing the things that got you there. Time after time, I work with habit creators who build habits, start to see results, and then strangely almost immediately slip back into old patterns. This is called the *licensing effect*.

An example of this is related to generosity. Strange survey results have found that if people give money to philanthropic causes, they are then found to be less generous in other circumstances. The reason for that is that they have "checked the box" for generosity mentally. They say, "Yes, I'm a generous person," and then give themselves license to act in ways that are less generous in other aspects of their lives. You see the same thing in dieting. When people go on diets, they will often get close to their goal weight only to then abandon those healthy behaviors, slip back into the old patterns, and immediately start increasing their weight. They give themselves license to stop continuing to engage in the behaviors that helped them lose weight. Be aware of the licensing effect because as you start making progress mentally, you may subconsciously check the box and believe that you are done when, in fact, you are not.

Scan this QR code for a video explaining the impact of the Licensing Effect.

As you start making progress, it's time to reemphasize the commitment to the behaviors to avoid the licensing effect. Acknowledge that the reason you're making progress is because of the new behaviors. Slipping back into the old behaviors will bring back the old results. When you feel the pull of the licensing effect, this is the time to connect with your celebration circle – both the people you have connected with in your personal sphere as well as the community of people online. Reengaging with your community will help you to recommit to the actions necessary for continued growth and happiness. As you push through this critical time you are likely to see increases in happiness, fulfillment, productivity, and satisfaction with your personal relationships. You may also experience changes in your emotional and mental state, your work performance as well as hobbies and other activities. There might be improvements in your health and your financial position.

All of these outcomes are highly likely when you commit to the process of habit improvement. Expect them and acknowledge them as they happen. Give yourself credit for the work you've done to get there. These changes are not coincidence or luck, they are because you have chosen to put in the consistent and intentional work to see those results. Be proud of the work you've done and be humble enough to know that you can continue to get those results as long as you continue to engage in the intentional work of making and sustaining positive habits. As you continue to grow happier and more fulfilled, engage with your celebration circle and your community. Talk about your success and the joy that you're feeling. When you share your success with others, your progress will inspire others to join you in this journey.

The only thing better than working on this journey is to work on this journey with someone else. Expect powerful results. ***There is an African proverb that says if you want to go fast, go alone, if you want to go far go together.*** You are not on this habit journey alone! There is a community of people who want to help you and with whom you can accelerate your progress so that you experience greater success.

Part of this habit journey can be the Happier Habits Mastermind group, made up of people just like you who want to go further. Along with me, they realized that working alone is not the path to success, nor is it the happiest way to live your habit journey. I invite you to go to www.thejasonharwood.com and click the link to find out more about the Happier Habits Mastermind and see if it's a fit for you. As part of the group, you will receive a series of habit trainings to reestablish these principles and recommit to consistently living by the three steps to habit formation.

More importantly, you'll tie into a community of people you can talk with monthly to share ideas, successes, failures, and setbacks; brainstorm possibilities and connect in ways unlike any other group you may be part of in other aspects of your life. You can go on the habit journey alone and if you are living the principles taught in this book, you will have success. But you may go faster in the Happier Habits Mastermind because when you work together in a community, your likelihood of success increases.

Whether you join the Happier Habits Mastermind or not, from here on out expect to live a happier life. Expect things to be better. Expect greater light in your day and greater feelings of peace and joy. Expect to feel better about yourself. Your circumstances may not change. You will probably end up living in the same house (at least for a while) with the same job, the same relationships, and the same external factors. But as soon as you start changing small behaviors, expect powerful results. I was in a dark place, and I used these exact principles to get to a place of greater happiness and light. I know that many people are in a similarly dark place, and the best I can do is teach you these principles that brought me happiness and light.

In this book, I have tried to give you the roadmap, set your feet on the path, point you in the right direction, and give you all the encouragement I can to walk down the path toward happiness and the light of joy. I hope this book helps you to move away from the darkness that may surround you, take one small and easy step, and celebrate. Then take another small, easy step and celebrate. As you find joy and the people in your celebration circle find joy, you will get closer to experiencing the full light and happiness of successful, consistent habits. For me, it really is that simple – even if it isn't easy at first.

I look forward to walking with you on the habit path and celebrating with you as you take one small easy step after another today so you can live happier and in the light of joy today.

Your Happily Ever After doesn't come because you hope for it. It comes when you create your own Happily Ever Habits!

About the Author

Jason Harwood is an author, speaker, and host of the *Happily Ever Habits* podcast. For over 20 years Jason has worked with individuals and businesses to create the systems and habits that lead to success and happiness.

Jason has an M.Ed. and is an award-winning speaker who has spoken around the world for small businesses as well as billion-dollar organizations. He has taught thousands of people to grow businesses while also building a happy life.

He currently lives in Idaho with his wife, endlessly chasing and taxiing his seven children.

Acknowledgments

Dedicated to:

Brooke for giving my life happiness.

J, H, T, A, T, C, and Z for giving my life purpose.

And to my mom for giving me life.

Made in United States
Troutdale, OR
10/19/2023

13835974R00053